Description and History of the »Great Eastern«

Description and History of the »Great Eastern«

ISBN/EAN: 9783954272655
Erscheinungsjahr: 2013
Erscheinungsort: Bremen, Deutschland

© maritimepress in Europäischer Hochschulverlag GmbH & Co. KG, Fahrenheitstr. 1, 28359 Bremen. Alle Rechte beim Verlag und bei den jeweiligen Lizenzgebern.

www.maritimepress.de | office@maritimepress.de

Bei diesem Titel handelt es sich um den Nachdruck eines historischen, lange vergriffenen Buches. Da elektronische Druckvorlagen für diese Titel nicht existieren, musste auf alte Vorlagen zurückgegriffen werden. Hieraus zwangsläufig resultierende Qualitätsverluste bitten wir zu entschuldigen.

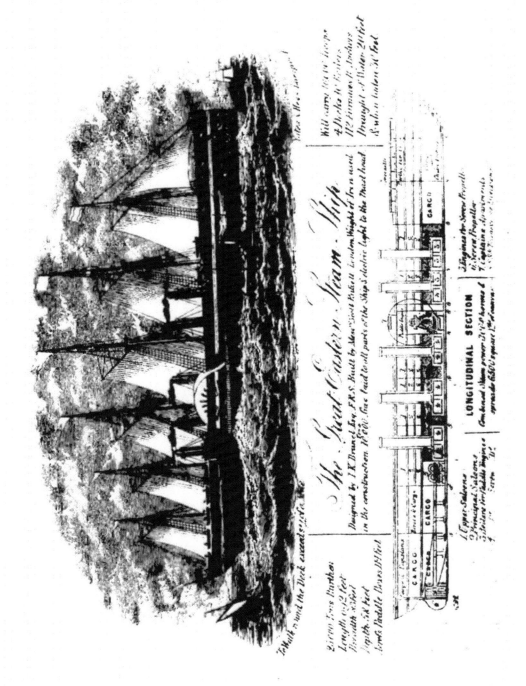

ADVERTISEMENT.

This little Book, descriptive of the " wonder of the world " and " of the deep,"—" The Great Eastern,"—has become necessary in consequence of the disposal of the majority of those numerous other works of a like nature, published from time to time, both in America and Great Britain. It contains many things new, but is in great part compiled from preceding treatises on the " Great Ship." It is hoped that it may serve as a guide to those who visit her, and interest those who cannot avail themselves of a personal inspection. It is sure to be valuable as a reliable source of reference for the time to come.

July, 1861.

TABLE OF CONTENTS.

	PAGES.
Advertisement	1
What suggested the Great Ship	3
Her size, material and estimated cost	4
The Company	4
The Hull and its construction	5
Description of the Hull	7
The time occupied in its construction	8
Noah's Ark and the Great Eastern	8
Launch	9
Departure of the Ship from the Thames	10
An Explosion on Board	11
Material.—Extent.—Accommodation	13
Passenger Accommodation	14
Steam Power and Engines	14
Propeller	15
The Screw Boilers	16
The Screw Propeller and Engine	17
Number of Anchors	17
Her Canvas	17
Her Saloons and Cabins	17
The Upper Deck	19
Her Seagoing Qualities	20
Rate of Sailing	21
At New York	21
The Great Eastern in the Mersey	21
Note of a Voyage from New York	22
The Great Eastern chartered by Government	27
She Sails for Canada.—Her Captain	28
Abstract of the Log	28
Business Cards	30

THE GREAT EASTERN.

What suggested the Great Ship.

It is probably some ten years since the question of Ocean Steam Navigation was discussed in the "British Association for the advancement of Science," with a view to the suggestion of some means by which Steam propulsion might be applied with similar effect to the Eastern Empire and Australian Colonies of Great Britain, as had been done in Trans-Atlantic communication. Some twenty years before Mr. Brunel, the eminent Engineer, had suggested the idea of the "Great Western," the first Steamer which was ever constructed for regular communication between Europe and America. He was consulted, and through him it was felt that if possible the idea would be realized. Soon after a Parliamentary Committee was appointed to consider the question, and "The Eastern Steam Navigation Company" was established, with a direct view of superseding, to a great extent, the "Peninsular and Oriental Navigation Company," which it was complained did not give the nation any adequate return for the immense subsidy, and, indeed, monopoly it enjoyed. The Committee reported in favor of competition with the Peninsular and Oriental Company, but the issue was a renewal of the contract with the latter, for a fortnightly mail from the East, which has now been quickened into one each week.

In the course of the investigations which then were made, it was known that the sea route by the Cape of Good Hope, was the shortest route to India, and there seemed good reason to conclude, that could a steamship be constructed so powerful and of such capacity that she could be relied on to make 18 to 20 miles an hour, and carry her own coal for the whole voyage, in addition to a proportionate cargo, the problem of the quickest route would probably still have its solution by way of the Cape. These are the *desiderata* then to which the constructive genius of Mr. Brunel was directed, and the "Great Eastern" was intended for the Indian and Australian route *viâ* the Cape of Good Hope.

The investigations and calculations of the Engineer led him to the conclusion, that the most suitable vessel for voyages of such length, would be one which equalled in capacity the distance out and home, fixed the tonnage of the "Great Eastern" at 22,500 tons, the route to Australia and back, being as nearly as possible 22,500 miles. Such a ship would be able to carry, with her fuel for the whole journey, besides furnishing enormous stowage room, and an extent and quality of passenger accommodation, which those who necessarily pass through the Tropics on ship board can best appreciate.

Her size, material and estimated cost.

The idea once suggested was adopted by "The Eastern Steam Navigation Company," and to Mr. Brunel was of course committed the labour of the designs. The material to be used was iron, and the estimated cost £804,522. A spot of ground was chosen on the banks of the Thames, in the building yard of the Company at Millwall, and the building was commenced, on the lines laid down by Mr. Scott Russell, on 1st May, 1854. Her cost to the present time has been estimated at £1,800,000.

The Company.

The Company was originally formed with a nominal capital of £1,200,000, power to augment to two millions being taken. The Chairman was Mr. R. J. Roy Campbell, a gentleman of extensive personal and mercantile connexion with India, and to him and Mr. G. T. Braine were committed the duty of examining, for approval or otherwise, the plans of Mr. Brunel and the lines of Mr. Scott Russell. The result of their investigation satisfied those gentlemen that, if the combinations proposed could be carried out, of which the scientific originators had no doubt, the enterprise must be an undoubted commercial success. As time passed on, however, and the ship made progress, difficulties arose in the path of the project, and for a time the plans were perilled by monetary embarrassments. Mr. Campbell, who felt no doubt a pride in being connected with one of the proudest speculations, scientifically as well as commercially, that the world had ever known, at this juncture energetically came forward to the rescue, and the "Great Ship Company" was formed, under whose auspices the labours of Brunel and Russell were brought to completion. But it is necessary with reference to dates to state, that while the change of companies was yet incomplete, the process of launching was begun, and after some months delay, completed. And now having said so much about the inception and realization of this magnificent vessel, we shall return somewhat upon the efflux of time, and enter on some details of her extent, construction and accommodations.

The Hull and its construction.

Every minute detail of the arrangements and building of this wonder of the world is fraught with interest. The mere preparing of the ground to receive her enormous weight was calculated to fill the minds of men with astonishments, Her supports and scaffoldings, and the machinery by which she was ultimately launched, taxed the skill of her engineers even more than her construction. A very town of workshops, foundries, and forges, sprang into being round her hull, and as this rose, foot by foot, in all its gigantic proportions the surrounding edifices dwindled down into insignificance, and the busy population of artificers clustered upon her like ants upon a prostrate monarch of the forest trees.

The ground on which the ship was built consisted of a layer of mud, about 30 feet thick, lying on a bed of gravel. Upwards of 1400 piles were driven into this ground. The first plate was laid on the first of May, 1854. This is a corresponding act in ship structure to the laying a foundation stone of a building, or turning the first sod of a railway. First, the keelplate was laid along on a level platform, prepared for it out of balks of timber about five feet from the ground ; then was fitted the centre web, which answers a little to the keel of an ordinary ship, only that it is put inside instead of outside, so that, strictly speaking, the Great Eastern has no keel. Then came other plates, laid flat on the top of the centre web, the three together making a figure like the letter H laid on its side thus I. Two poles or derricks, 100 feet long, were placed one on each side of the ship, wherever a bulk head was to be built. Platforms were hung in a longitudinal direction, from which the inner and outer skin and web were put in their places. Four square towers of open timber framework, with staircases up them, were also built, two on each side. They were intended as gangways, from which the workmen could get on or off the ship. From these platforms, plate after plate, as it was brought already prepared was fitted into its place, and so accurate were the calculations and workmanship that every plate fitted and all the holes in each new plate came exactly right for those preceding. Thus gradually grow the bulkheads, and the sides of the inner vessel closed over them, next were fixed the webs and outside the exterior hull of the vessel. The bow and stern being at length reached and finished revealed the beautiful proportions of " The Great Eastern."

There is properly no keel to the " Great Eastern " but in its place a flat keel-plate of iron 2 feet wide and 1 inch thick which runs the entire length from stem to stern.

This is the base upon which all the rest is reared. The iron plates which form her planking are $\frac{3}{4}$ of an inch thick. Up to the water-mark the hull is constructed with an inner and outer skin, 2 feet 10 inches apart, both skins being made of ¾ inch plates, except at the bottom, where the plates are an inch thick; and between these, at intervals of 6 feet, run horizontal webs of iron plates, which bind the two skins together, and thus it may be said that the lower part of the hull is 2 feet 10 inches thick. This mode of construction adds materially to the safety of the vessel; for, in the event of a collision at sea, the outer skin might be pierced while the inner remained intact. The space may also at any time be filled with water, and thus ballast, to the amount of 2500 tons, may be obtained.

Some idea of the magnitude and weight of the vessel may be formed from the fact, that each iron plate weighs about ⅓ of a ton, and is fastened with 100 iron rivets. About 30,000 of these plates have been used in her construction, and 3,000,000 rivets. The fastening of these rivets was one among the many curious operations performed in course of building. The riveting men were arranged in gangs, each gang consisting of two riveters, one holder-up, and three boys. Two boys were stationed at the fire or portable forge, and one with the holder up. This boy's duty was to receive the red-hot rivet with his pincers from the boy at the forge, and insert it in the hole destined for its reception, the point protruding about an inch. The holder-up immediately placed his heavy hammer against the head of the rivet and held it firmly there, while the two riveters assailed it in front with alternate blows, until the countersunk part of the hole was filled up, after which the protruding head was cut off smooth with the plate; the whole operation scarce occupying a minute. In riveting the double part of the ship, the holder-up and his boy were necessarily in the interior part of the tubes, and passed the whole day in the narrow space between (2 feet 10 inches wide) in the total darkness, except the glimmer afforded by a single dip candle, and immediately under the deafening blows of the riveters.

There are two large holds, to be devoted exclusively to cargo, one at each end of the cabins. They are both 60 feet long, and are the whole depth and breadth of the ship; each is capable of holding about 1,000 tons of cargo. The total quantity of space appropriated to cargo will be regulated entirely by circumstances. It would be quite easy to stow 6,000 tons in the hold and various other unappropriated places. The crew and officers are berthed fore and aft. The captain has a splendid suite of rooms on deck, within easy distance of the paddle-boxes.

The Great Eastern has twenty ports on the lower deck, each 5 ft. square, to receive railway-waggons. They are 5 feet above the water level when the vessel is loaded, but are perfectly water-tight. The bulwarks are 10 feet high forward, and slope down to 4 feet 9 inches amidships. The massive wrought-iron deck is covered with teak planking, placed about 6 inches distance from the iron. The weight of the whole ship when voyaging, with every contemplated article and person on board, will be not less than 25,000 tons.

Description of the Hull.

The ship is divided by transverse bulkheads into twelve perfectly water-tight compartments below and nine above the lower deck, so that, should the inner skin by any chance be fractured, the water would only flow into that compartment where the damage occurred, and no danger to the ship would arise if ever two of these compartments were completely filled with water. Moreover, if the ship were actually cut in two, both portions would float. Besides these transverse bulkheads, there are two others which extend from the bottom of the ship to the upper deck, and run longitudinally for a length of 350 feet, thus dividing the ship transversely into three separate compartments. Where these exist, the machinery, boilers, and coal are placed below the lower deck, and the cabins above. Forward and aft the space is devoted to cargo, rooms for officers and crews, chains and capstans. There are also two tubular iron platforms, extending from the gunwale to the longitudinal bulkheads, which are 36 ft. apart, and running right fore and aft. These are connected together about every 60 ft. by iron platforms, 7 feet wide. The bow and stern are plated right across. To the construction of the bow great attention has been paid. Every deck has been plated across for 60 feet, and several iron platforms and vertical webs have been inserted between the two skins to make the ship capable, as far as possible, of resisting any impediment, such as ice, which it may encounter. Several iron platforms and vertical webs have been placed in the sterns, and every thing that forethought could suggest has been done to render it capable of resisting the constant vibration of the screw, which represent a force of 1600 horses constantly trying to shake it. The iron plates, of which the whole of the outside skin of the ship is made, are $\frac{3}{4}$ of an inch thick, except the keel plates which is one inch thick. The average size of these plates, is about 10 feet long by 2 feet 9 inches wide, each plate weighing about 825 lbs. There were one or two enormous plates required for the sternpost and keel, two of these were 27 feet long by 3 feet 3 inch wide, $1\frac{1}{4}$ inch thick, weighing about 2 tons, the others were 25 feet long by 4 feet wide, and $1\frac{1}{4}$ inch thick. The tubular iron decks, running along the top of the ship, are composed of double half inch plates at the top and bottom of the tubes, and webs 1 foot 9 inches deep and half an inch thick, running between them. The total number of plates used in the construction of the hull is about 30,000, of an average weight of nearly 600 lbs. each. Rivets, 1 inch and $\frac{7}{8}$ inch diameter, have been used about 3 inches apart, where it was necessary to make it watertight, in other places from 4 inches to 8 inches. Assuming 60 rivets were used for each plate, the total number of rivets used would be nearly 2,000,000. These were all inserted and hammered while at white heat. The total weight of iron in the hull is about 8,000 tons.

The time occupied in its construction.—On the first of May, 1854, the building of the Great Eastern commenced, and in August, 1859, it was completed. Thus occupying the space of 5 years and 3 months in its construction, one year and five months more than was required for the erection of the Britannia Tubular Bridge. The mere painting of the vessel, slight as the fact may appear when mentioned, involves a labour of no common magnitude, for the painted surface of the ship is, inside and outside, nearly 120,000 square yards in extent, or more than 24 acres! Ocean steam navigation seems to be indebted for almost every thing to Brunel; he was the architect of the Great Western, the first steamer that crossed the Atlantic; also of the Great Britain, the first steamer in which the screw proved its preeminence over the paddle, and in which iron showed itself preferable to wood, and now he completes his work by building a vessel capable of performing the circuit of the earth by means of steam. The magnificent range of saloons and sleeping rooms are divided into different sets or "hotels," between which there is no communication except by the upper deck. Each hotel has its own saloons, bedrooms, kitchen, and bar, and is conducted independently of the other. It is only by some such arrangement that 4,000 guests could be properly served. The sleeping rooms are 14 feet long, by 7 or 8 feet wide, and about 7 feet high. If nothing else had influence, this would make the Great Eastern popular. In most large steamers it is the sleeping cabin that is the discomfort. The main cabin is generally large and airy, the table perhaps better than many passengers have on shore,—it is in the berth that they find discomfort. It will require between 40 and 50 servants, to work 6 hours a day, merely to arrange the sleeping apartments.

Noah's Ark and the Great Eastern.—The following is a comparison between the size of Noah's Ark and the Great Eastern, both being considered in point of tonnage after the old law for calculating the tonnage.

The sacred "cubit," as stated by Sir Isaac Newton, is 20·625 English inches; by Bishop Wilkins, 21·88 inches. According to these authorities the dimensions are as follows:—

	Sir I. Newton. English Feet.	Bishop Wilkins. English Feet.	Great Eastern. English Feet.
Length between perpendiculars.	515·62	547·0	680·0
Breadth	85·94	91·16	83·0
Depth	51·56	54·70	60·0
Keel, or length for tonnage	464·08	492·31	630·2
Tonnage according to old law	18,231 58-94	21,761 50-94	23,092 25-94

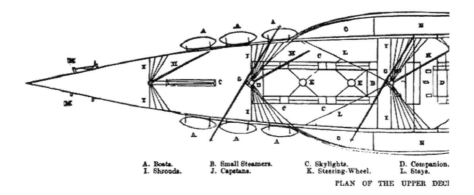

A. Boats. B. Small Steamers. C. Skylights. D. Companion.
I. Shrouds. J. Capstans. K. Steering-Wheel. L. Stays.

PLAN OF THE UPPER DECK

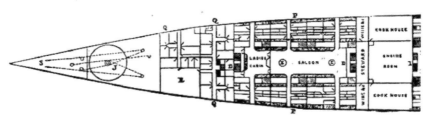

PLAN SHOWING THE PASSENGER AC[COMMODATION]

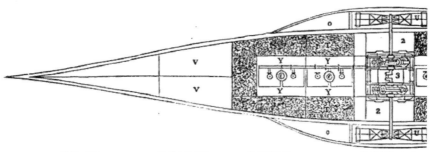

E. Funnels. O. The Sponson. T. Coal Bunkers. U. Paddle-wheel.
Z. Tunnels through the Coal Bunkers. 1. Propeller Engine. 2. Cook House.

PLAN SHOWING THE ARRANGEMENT OF T[HE]

LONGITUDINAL SECTION OF THE GREAT EAS[TERN]

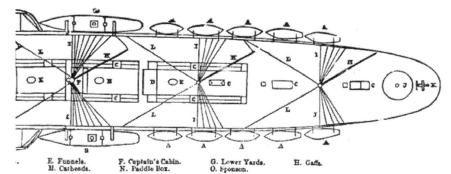

E. Funnels.　　F. Captain's Cabin.　　G. Lower Yards.　　H. Gaffs.
M. Catheads.　　N. Paddle Box.　　O. Sponson.

K OF THE GREAT EASTERN.

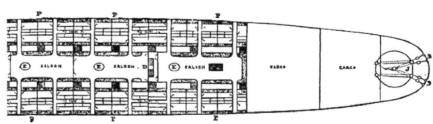

COMMODATION OF THE GREAT EASTERN.

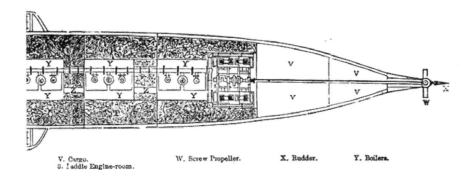

V. Cargo.　　W. Screw Propeller.　　X. Rudder.　　Y. Boilers.
S. Paddle Engine-room.

THE MACHINERY OF THE GREAT EASTERN.

TERN, SHOWING THE INTERNAL ARRANGEMENTS.

In 1837, the "Great Western," (under the auspices of Isambard Kingdom Brunel, Esqr.,—the father of transatlantic navigation, and whose triumphs in steam navigation have given him world-wide celebrity), was completed, measuring 236 feet in length by 36 in width, of 1,350 tons, with two engines, 225 horse power. The germ of the Great Eastern was thus evidently grafted on that gentleman's fertile and versatile brain. After this the "Duke of Wellington," 240 feet in length by 61 in breadth. Then the "British Queen," 275 feet in length by 61 in width. Then the "Great Britain," 322 feet by 51. Then the "Himalaya," 370 feet by 43. At the time of her construction she was the largest iron screw steamer in the world, and the finest specimen of the application of the screw-propeller. This noble vessel conveyed 418 troops and 372 horses from Liverpool to Constantinople, a distance of 3,620 miles, in a little over 12 days, although she partly lay-to through stress of weather between Cape St. Vincent and Gibraltar. Then the "Persia" was launched, and astonished the world by her noble proportions, and eventually by her splendid speed. She was 390 feet in length, and 45 in width,—the largest paddle steamer afloat. She has made the journey to America in less than 10 days, the quickest passage on record.

Launch.—The first attempt, which was made on Tuesday, November 3rd, 1857, to launch this stupendous vessel, by letting her sideways down the ways into the river, proved unsuccessful, from the breaking away of a part of the ingenious construction, owing to the enormous weight of the ship. The thousands who flocked to see the Great Ship make her first plunge, were vastly disappointed by the monster of the deep remaining fast, and refusing to take to the water; and Mr. Brunel was blamed on all hands for a failure which the accusing parties did not understand, and which they were entirely incompetent to mend. The attempt was renewed again and again, but with very little success. On the 28th of November the vessel moved some five and twenty feet, and it was evident the launch was merely a work of time. For some time this queen of the seas had remained sulky and silent, firm in her two cradles, and seeming to frown contemptuously upon the gazing crowd below; till at length, by varied manœuvres, she was coaxed into a good humour, and casting her hesitency to the winds, she at once made up her mind, for better or for worse, to be united to her expectant and wooing partner. The breeze gently pressed her bosom with a farewell kiss as she placidly and majestically glided from our shores for ever into her future home, amidst the hearty congratulations of assembled thousands, who witnessed the consummation so devoutly wished. This long-looked-for event took place January 31, 1858. When the announcement "It's afloat" was made, it drew forth the most hearty cheering from the vast multitude, and when the mighty ship was seen gliding smoothly as a swan to her moorings the cheering was renewed. It is very gratifying to know that notwithstanding two months' hauling and lugging, and the application of immense pressure, the Great Eastern has not sustained the slightest blemish, and that her "shear" is as free from defect as before the launch was attempted.

Departure of the Ship from the Thames.

The day fixed for the vessel leaving her moorings at Deptford was Wednesday, the 7th of September, 1859. At four o'clock on that morning all hands were astir and busied in the necessary preparations. Half a dozen tugs were brought up and made fast to the huge vessel, four being lashed alongside and the remaining two attached by long hawsers to her bows. The whole of the arrangements were completed soon after seven. The time of high water was ten minutes before ten; but it was thought that in the event of the ship touching ground the rising tide would be of material assistance. At half-past seven Mr. Atkinson, the pilot, gave the word "Let slip the moorings!" It should be stated that these moorings consisted of three huge chains passing through hawse-holes at the head and a similar number passing through hawseholes at the stern of the vessel, all six being made fast to "bits" inside. When, therefore, the chains were cast off, their weight caused them to quit the ship with surprising velocity, and to emit not so much a shower of sparks as a perfect blaze of flame, accompanied by a roar that must have been heard almost as far as the tolling of the great Westminster bell. It is hardly an exaggeration to say that they announced, as with a salvo of artillery, that the Great Eastern was free. The tugs began to make way, and, the ship's own screw being put into requisition, the vessel glided majestically from her berth. The spectacle appeared to afford the multitude, who lined both banks of the river, the liveliest gratification, for they cheered with a lustiness and a perseverance that have seldom been exceeded. After a short time, however, an awkward turn into Blackwall Reach was approached, and the plaudits of the spectators now gave way to a feeling of intense anxiety. There was a stiff breeze blowing S. S. W., and the force which this must necessarily exert on her huge broadside rendered it more than doubtful whether the ship would be able to round the corner without going ashore. Amongst the nautical men present, "e'en the boldest held his breath for a time." Happily their fears proved groundless. The vessel, in the words of her pilot, "steered like a boat;" and in the skilful hands in which she was the danger was quickly passed. Hearty cheers told how warmly the marine population sympathised with her happy escape. The vessel was opposite Blackwall Pier at about half-past eight. Presently a new danger showed itself ahead. The harbourmaster had on the previous day given strict orders that all craft should be moved out of the vessel's path; but, lo! a large barque was found lying right in the middle of her course. At first a collision seemed inevitable; but the coolness and skill of the pilot, who was ably seconded by Captain Harrison, the master, were once more equal to the emergency. There remains little to add with regard to the rest of the day's journey beyond the fact that all along the river she received a perfect ovation from myriads of sympathising spectators. The ship was kept clear of all shoals and sharp angles, and by about eleven o'clock she arrived at Purfleet, which is at the commencement of Long Reach. Here Mr. Atkinson, with the full concurrence of Captain Harrison, determined to stop. The starboard bow anchor (one of Trotman's patent) was let go with forty fathoms of chain cable, and it immediately brought up the immense floating mass. By this time the tide was running out, and the vessel, slowly canting round, remained firmly fixed, with her head up stream.

On the following morning the anchor was again weighed, and the ship proceeded on her way; and, although under every possible disadvantage arising from the necessarily imperfect nature of her trim, she exhibited powers of speed, and steadiness on the water, tested as she was by a smart gale of wind which she had to encounter, which surpassed all the expectations, great as they were, which had been formed of her capabilities. From Purfleet to the Nore all went well, and more than well. On the morning of Friday she proceeded on her way, neither pitching, rolling or vibrating, amidst weather which compelled every other craft which came within sight of her either to run for safety into some harbour, or to labour and struggle with the storm in a manner that appeared alarming, at least to the landsmen, who, undisturbed and at their ease on the deck of the Great Eastern, watched the less happy condition of the ordinary skimmers of the seas. As a proof of the gentle movement of the ship it may be mentioned that, while she was in motion, and her engines, both paddle and screw, at the highest speed which they were allowed to attain, Mr. Nottage, of the London Stereoscopic Company, who was specially authorized by the Directors to take a series of photographs connected with the vessel, was employed in that duty without disturbance or hindrance. The peril of the Goodwin Sands was securely weathered, Dover was passed, and all was going on so well, and under such favourable circumstances, the weather having cleared up, the wind abated, and the speed of the vessel something marvellous, that it was supposed she would arrive in Portland Roads that night.

An Explosion on Board.

At six o'clock the ship was off Hastings, at about seven miles distance from the shore. The passengers had just concluded dinner, the ladies were on their way from the dining saloon to the grand saloon, and lingered on the deck, when the verberation of a tremendous explosion was heard, followed by a crash and the scattering fall of fragments of wood, iron and glass. It is only necessary to state here that the forward funnel had burst, owing to the simple and minute circumstance that a safety-valve attached to the casing had been neglected. Captain Harrison, the commander of the vessel, at once lowered himself into the grand salooon, through which the funnel passed, and which was, of course, seriously injured, and ascertained that no one, except a little girl, his own daughter, was in that part of the ship, and she was in safety. Mr. Campbell, the managing director, remained calm and collected on deck, getting the crew forward and preventing any unnecessary alarm. Search was instantly made for those employed in the stokeholes, all of whom were brought up, several more or less injured, and some of them, unfortunately, mortally hurt. Melancholy as was this catastrophe, accompanied as it was by loss of life and serious damage to the internal fittings of the vessel, it is impossible not to recognise the fact, that in no other ship and under no other circumstances could such an accident have occurred attended with such comparatively small consequences. Had Mr. Brunel proposed, while she lay at Deptford, and before any fittings were in, to deck over and fit up with rough model of cabins, floors, &c., &c., one of the compartments, and then, by way of testing her power of endurance, to explode in the bottom of that compartment a charge of gunpowder sufficient to hoist one of her huge funnels fifty feet in to the air, it may be supposed that the proposal would have been received with very considerable astonishment and demur on the part of directors, shareholders and every one interested in her welfare; and yet this is, in fact, what the recent accident has effected. An explosion took place in one of the compartments, the certain effects of which on any other ship that ever was constructed, may be gathered from the significant fact that the first impulse of an experienced navigator, Captain Comstock, who was on board, was to spring on the paddle-box and look over the sides, to see if they were blown out. No other ship afloat could have withstood the enormous bursting pressure of the steam, nor have survived the shock; and yet it is a literal and actual fact that *no harm whatever* has been done to any part of the fabric. The sides, the bulkheads, and every portion of the frame remain in their former imperturbable rigidity; whilst in the next compartment, but one, the shock experienced was no more, as one of the gentlemen present expressed it, than if one of the crew passing overhead with a twelve-pound shot in his hands had let it fall on the deck. There was no need to stop the vessel's course. Her engines continued to work as before, and on her arrival in Portland harbour she was ready to be thrown open to visitors—excepting, of course, the parts under repair.

Material.—Extent.—Accommodation.

Length (between perpendiculars)	680 ft
Length (on the upper deck)	691 ft
Breadth	83 ft
Breadth (across the paddle-boxes)	118 ft
Depth (from deck to keel)	58 ft
Depth of hull	83 ft
Number of decks	4
Number of masts	6
Number of boats	20
Quantity of canvas under full sail	6,500 sq yds
Weight of ship, with machinery, coal, cargo, &c.	26,000 tons
Draught of water at that weight	30 ft 6 in.
Draught of water unladen	15 ft 6 in.
Number of anchors	10
Length of chain cable 800 fathoms, or	4,800 ft
Weight of anchors, cables, &c	253 tons
Nominal horse-power of paddle engines	1,200
Number of boilers for paddle engines	4
Weight of each boiler	50 tons
Number of furnaces for paddle engines	40
Nominal horse-power of screw engines	1,600
Number of boilers to screw engines	6
Weight of each boiler	57 tons
Number of furnaces to screw engines	72
Plates of iron used the in construction of the hull	30,000
Number of rivets used in fastening the plates	3,000,000
(One million more than were used at Britannia Tubular Bridge.)	
Weight of iron used in the construction of the hull, (about)	10,000 tons
(1,366 tons less than used at the Britannia Bridge)	
Number of auxiliary engines	4
Ditto donkey engines	10
Number of screw steamers abaft paddle boxes	2
Length of screw steamers	100 ft
Nominal horse-power of ditto	40
Thickness of iron plates in keel	1 inch
Thickness of iron plat in the skin	¾ inch
Thickness of plates in the bulkheads	½ inch
Thickness of iron deck	½ inch

Passenger Accommodation.

1st class, 800 ; 2nd class, 2,000 ; 3rd class, 1,200 ; total	4,000
Accommodation for troops alone, about............	10,000
Number of Saloons................................	10
Length of principal Saloon.....	62 ft
Width of ditto........	36 ft
Height of ditto....	12 ft
Length of berths......	14 ft
Width of ditto	10 ft
Height of ditto.................................	7 ft

Steam Power and Engines.

The distinguishing feature in the character of the Great Eastern, in addition to her vast size, is the combined application of steam power through the paddle-wheel and the screw. The engines are very considerably larger than any hitherto made for marine purposes, and their actual power will be very far greater than their nominal power. The vessel has ten boilers and five funnels, and each boiler can be cut off from its neighbour, and used or not as desired. The boilers are placed longitudinally along the centre of the ship, and entirely independent of each other. Each boiler (weighing 45 tons) has ten furnaces, and that gives to the whole the large number of one hundred and twelve furnaces.

The engines for the screw-propeller are of 1,600 nominal horse-power. They were made by Messrs. James Watt and Co., Soho Works, Birmingham, and are supplied with steam by six of the boilers, working to a force of upwards of 5,000 horse-power. The screw-propeller, 24 feet in diameter, with fans or vanes, the largest ever made, is placed in the stern of the vessel, and is worked in the usual manner. The shaft is 150 feet in length and weighs 60 tons. Among other improvements, the screw-engines are furnished with " Silver's patent marine governors," which have been constructed and fitted by his agents, Messrs. J. Hamilton and Co., engineers, Glascow ; and, as their duty will be to regulate the supply of steam in accordance with the required power as the ship may pitch or roll about in a seaway, all danger of accident to the machinery and waste of steam arising from what is usually termed the " racing" of the engines will be avoided, and a uniform propulsion of the ship through the water will be secured. The want of such an appendage to the marine-engine has long been felt ; and, indeed, it is remarkable that, while the smallest stationary engine has long since been provided with a governor to regulate its speed according to the amount of work imposed upon it, the marine-engine has hitherto been left exposed to all these sudden changes of resistance by the screw or paddle rising out of, or dropping into, the water; that its movements are necessarily rendered exceedingly irregular, and frequently in rough weather give occasion for much uneasiness as to its safety, to say nothing of the actual wear, tear and waste of steam it thereby sustains.

The paddle-wheels, the diameter of which is 57 feet, with means provided for reducing the diameter, are worked by engines constructed by Mr. Scott Russell: they are direct-acting, with four oscillating cylinders, each 17 feet long, and 6 feet 2 inches in diameter. The stroke is 14 feet. These engines have a force of 1,000 nominal horse power, capable of being worked to 3,000 horse power the steam being generated by the remaining four boilers: they are constructed on the disconnecting principle; can be used separately or jointly and both or either paddle wheels can be made run free of the engine or put in independent motion.

The building of the paddle-engines was commenced about the same time as that of the ship. They were originally put together in the erecting-shop. The time thus occupied was about twelve months. They were then taken down, and re-erected in the ship. The actual time thus consumed was about four months, independently of various delays which occurred: including these, the building and erecting of the paddle-engines were going on simultaneously with the construction of the ship itself. There are also four auxiliary high-pressure engines, two of 10 horse-power and two of 25 horse-power. These engines are adapted to receive connections for working-pumps, and the necessary machinery for hoisting sails, weighing anchor, and other laborious tasks usually performed by sailors. There are besides thirteen small engines for filling the boilers and doing other work.

Propeller.

The Propeller Shaft intended to move the screw itself, is 160 feet in length, and weighs 60 tons; the after length of this shaft are 47 feet long and weigh 35 tons, was made at the Lancefield Forge; this portion of the shaft is the heaviest piece of wrought iron in the ship. The other lengths of the Propeller Shaft, consisting of different pieces, each 25 feet long and 16 tons weight, were made in London for Messrs. JAMES WATT and Co., the Builders of the Screw Engines.

The Screw Engines designed and built by Messrs. JAMES WATT & Co., of the Soho Works, are horizontal direct acting engines of

Nominal Horse Power	1600
Number of Cylinders	4
Diameter of each Cylinder	84-in.
Length of stroke	4-ft.
Number of revolutions per minute	50

These are the largest ever made for marine purposes; and, as in the case with the paddle cylinders, each of the four is in itself a complete and separate engine capable of working quite independent of the other three.

The combined Screw Engines work up to an indicator power of 4,500 horses of 33,000 lb. when working at 45 strokes a minute with steam in the boiler at 15lb., and the expansion valve cutting off at one third of the stroke, they are however made to work smoothly either at 40 strokes per minute, with steam at 25lb. without expansion, or at 55 strokes a minute with the expansion cutting off at one fourth of the stroke. Under these circumstances they will be working at the tremendous power of 6,500 horses.

The Screw Boilers.

The Boilers for the Screw Engines are similar to those for the paddle engines, but a trifle larger and heavier. They are ten in number, and the whole are so arranged that all or any of them can be used with either set of engines. The weight of the screw engines and boilers is 1500 tons. To communicate between the different stoke holes and engine rooms there are two perfectly watertight tubes, 6 feet high and 4 feet wide, running through the ship the openings into which can be closed by watertight doors. Through one of them the various steam pipes go, and the others are used as a passage for the Engineers and Stokers. There are ten Donkey Engines to pump water into the boilers, and two auxiliary high pressure engines of 70 horse power, these are connected with the screw shaft so as to enable them to drive the screw, if necessary, when disconnected from its main engine. The Paddle and Screw Engines when working together, at their highest power, will exert an effective force of not less than 11,500 horse power, or sufficient to raise 200,000 gallons of water per minute to the top of the Monument in London.

The Screw as a Steam-Motor.

In the year 1785 Joseph Bramah, the inventor of the hydraulic-press, locks, &c., took out a patent for an engine and a propeller for vessels, which he described as being like a smokejack, and which he called a "screw-propeller." This is the first mention ever made of this excellent contrivance. It was never tried; but the merit of its first invention was due to Mr. Bramah. Other patents were taken out after this; and Littleton, Shorter, and Brown, and Mr. Stevens, an American Gentleman, worked a boat with a contrivance of a similar nature. On the 19th of July, 1830, Capt. Erricson, of the Swedish Navy, patented an arrangement of the screw-propeller, and, after making a variety of experiments in the Thames, but which were not sufficient to induce our Government to adopt his plan, he went to the United States, where he successfully applied his screw-propeller to a number of vessels. On the 1st of May, 1836, Francis Pettit Smith obtained a patent for improvements in a screw-propeller, and in 1839 a company was formed for carrying out his plan. In 1845 the largest vessel that had then been constructed—the Great Britain—made her first voyage across the Atlantic, having been fitted with the screw-propeller and built of iron. Since then the screw has been adjusted in vessels of every size, in both mercantile craft and ships of war. The idea of combining the paddle and the screw in the same vessel is due to Mr. Brunel. Why it should not have occurred to any one before is difficult to see now; but the simplest conceptions are the property of great minds alone.

The Screw Propeller and Engine.

The screw propeller which is 24 feet in diameter and 44 feet pitch, is the largest ever made. The four fans wen cast separately, and afterwards fitted into a large cast iron boss. The weight of this screw is thirty-six tons.

Number of Anchors.

The number of anchors is ten, and the prodigious weight of them, and the 800 fathoms of chain-cable necessary for their service—together 253 tons—is in proportion to the other items.

The vessel will draw 32 feet of water when laden, 22 feet only when light. The speed of the vessel was estimated by Mr. Brunel at fifteen to twenty knots an hour, without diminution or cessation, under any weather, which would accomplish the voyage between England and Australia, *viâ* the Cape of Good Hope, in about thirty-three days, and to India in about thirty days; half the time occupied by the fastest clippers afloat.

Her Canvas.

The arrangements effected for the propulsion of the vessel, besides the aid of steam power, are as follow :—

She has six masts (three of the masts are of hollow wrought iron, and three of wood), the two principal being crossed by yards, as in a line-of-battle ship, the remainder being schooner-rigged; there are upwards of 6,500 square yards of canvas available. A bowsprit is dispensed with.

Some notion of the size of the yards may be formed when it is stated that, although in proportion to her size the ship is what is called jury-rigged, her main yards are 24 feet longer than were those of the Caledonia, the old first-rate man of war, which is now used for the well-known purposes of the hospital-ship which lies in the river off Grenwich.

Her Saloons and Cabins.

The chief saloon, which is situated forward of the engine-rooms, an advantage not usual in other ships, is 62 feet long by 36 feet wide, and 12 feet high;

adjoining it is the ladies' cabin, 20 feet long. The arrangements for ventilating and lighting the lower cabins from the skylight above necessitated the railing off of open space on each side of the saloon. Besides this, two of the enormous funnels find their way upwards through this room. These peculiarities all presented considerable difficulties to be overcome in the decoration. The open spaces on each side are treated as arcades, resting on light iron columns; and between these are ornamental balustrades, also of iron, of every delicate design. Both these were cast by the Coalbrookdale Iron Company, and are beautiful specimens of their work. This ironwork is all treated by a peculiar process in imitation of oxydised silver relieved with gilding.

Above are the columns which support, by means of brackets, the iron beams of the ship. There is no attempt at concealing these, but they are decorated alternately in blue and red, the under side being gilt. The spaces between these beams are divided into panels which are very lightly decorated in colour and gold.

The walls are hung with a rich pattern in raised gold and white, divided into panels by green stiles and pilasters in imitation of oxydised silver, to correspond with the columns.

The two large funnel casings, which occupy considerable space in the room, are octagon in plan. The four larger side of these have been covered with mirrors, which continue the perspective of the saloon, and almost do away with the appearance of obstruction which before existed. On the four smaller sides, at the angles, are arabesque panels ornamented with children and emblems of the sea.

Mirrors are also placed on the large airshafts at the sides of the saloon, and on each side of them are other arabesque paintings with children personifying the arts and sciences connected with the building and navigation of the ship.

There are portières of rich crimson silk to all the doorways; and the carpet, of which the pattern is simple, the prevailing colour being maroon, assists in giving effect to the other decorations.

The sofas are covered with Utrectht velvet, and the buffets are of walnut wood richly carved, the tops being of a fine green marble.

A very peculiar feature in this unique saloon is the mode by which it is lighted and ventilated at the sides—by large openings railed off with gilt balustrades, and reaching to the upper deck, where they are met by skylights, which can be left up or down at pleasure. Besides the great additional light which these openings give, they are invaluable as securing at any moment currents of fresh air—a luxury which will only be fully appreciated when the Great Eastern is steaming majestically across the Indian Ocean with her living freight of some eight or ten thousand passengers for Calcutta. Next to this imperial saloon is another and still longer one, which is to be appropriated to the ordinary first-class passengers, the other being exclusively devoted to the extra first and the ladies. Around these two principal saloons the sleeping-berths of the passengers are skilfully arranged, the amount of accommodation being regulated, of course, by the price paid for the passage. But it is hardly fair to call them mere berths, seeing that they are, generally speaking, rather suites of apartments, comprising sleeping, sitting and dressing rooms, all self-contained, and offering to females as complete seclusion as if they were in their own homes. The smallest of these berths is larger than the best cabins in any other vessel; and they have the peculiar advantage of being at least double the height, and possessing most ample and ready means of ventilation.

The cabins are not all arranged alike, but some are constructed as "family cabins," and some in the usual "two-and-two" fashion; whilst others, by a combination of both the above styles, can be turned into a suite of one large and two small ones, making up eight bed places altogether, all opening into each other, and capable of being shut out completely from the passage and the rest of the ship. Each family cabin measures 18 feet by 7 feet 6 inches, and is 7 feet 6 inches high, and is furnished with every necessary convenience. The berths are so constructed that by a very simple process they can be made to collapse and fold together against the sides of the cabin, leaving a space of six inches between the two, so as to admit of stowing away the bedclothes; this done, curtains are drawn across, and so kept until night, the consequence being not only that the bed arrangements are entirely concealed all day, and the cabin turned into a snug little drawing-room, but that space is gained equal to about one-third of the whole area. The tables are so arranged as to be capable of extension or diminution in size. The cabins are floored with oilcloth, with Turkey rugs above. Under one of the settees is a bath, which can be easily supplied with hot, fresh or salt water, by the aid of what are called the "donkey engines" or some of the multitudinous shaftings which are to work everything all over the ship. Some idea will be formed from this attempt at description of the accommodation for passengers afforded by the vessel and which are carried out on much the same scale in every class and department, the difference consisting nearly in the degree of plainness or ornamentation as the case may be.

The Upper Deck.

The deck of the ship is double or cellular; and its strength which is very great to a considerable degree depends upon its construction which is on the plan of Stephensons great work, the Britannia tubular bridge. The formation is in this way: there on two half inch plates at bottom and two at top and those are supported by webs the whole running the length of the ship so that the deck which is of teak planking placed over the top plates forms the upper surface of the tube.

The bulwarks which add considerably both to the height and symmetrical proportions of the vessel, are 9 feet 6 inches high forward, and slope down to about 5 feet high, amidships and aft.

The upper deck runs flush and clear from stem to stern for a breadth of about twenty feet on either side, thus affording two magnificent promenades for the passengers just within the bulwarks. These promenades are rather more than the eighth of a mile long. Four turns up and down either side of them exceed a mile by 256 feet.

Between the two side promenades of the upper deck, are low bulwarks to which are fixed the sky lights of the large saloons for passengers. These saloons are forty-two feet wide, and nearly sixty feet long, the longest being one hundred feet, and there are deck gangways connecting the side promenades, between each of them.

This deck has been planned to be of such strength, that if the ship were taken up by its two extremities and the entire weight the vessel is ever to carry were hung upon its middle, it would sustain the whole by its unaided powers of resistance.

Her Seagoing Qualities.

The easy motion of the ship may be understood when I state that many of the passengers spent the whole day on the lower deck playing skittles. Another proof of the extraordinary ease with which the ship rolls is the fact that several tumblers stood the whole day and night on a polished marble table in the smoking room without being thrown down. * * * A moderate swell rolling across the bosom of the Atlantic the great ship acknowledging its presence by rolling very easily and in a most dignified manner or as the sailors express it "taking her time about it" * * * The ship is labouring under every disadvantage being some six feet by the stern and having a very foul bottom which with the deficiency of steam tends materially to decrease her speed * * * [The "decrease" here spoken of refers to a 5 lbs pressure taken off the safety valve previous to leaving Southampton.] * * It is worthy of remark that there has been a total absence among the passengers of that terrible nausea sea-sickness; for during the whole voyage we have not had one case even among the ladies. The paddle engines had a pressure on their boilers of 20lbs and the wheel was revolving 12 times per minute. The ship was headed to the Westward and there was experienced for the first time the heavy ground swell, and for ever set at rest, if such was ever entertained by any individual on board that a ship can be built large enough to resist the swell of the ocean *

The whole day she has been rolling about 25 degrees each way proving beyond doubt that she can roll much the same as an ordinary vessel in the event of encountering a heavy sea * * Unsecured articles of furniture replace themselves with wonderful alacrity and two of the saloon chandeliers suddenly sought the deck in unceremonious haste. But due allowance must be made for the empty state of her inside.

Rate of Sailing.

The "big Ship" performed the distance between Halifax and Milford Haven" 2357 miles less difference of time in 168h. 45m. or 13. 95 knots per hour being nearly 16 statute miles. Received a visit at New York from Mr. Jacobs (the Wizard); among his friends was one "old English gentleman" whom we had invited to view the Great Eastern by moonlight. Never shall I forget his extacy when he stood upon her spacious quarter deck; but after ascending to the top of the paddle box "hold my hat and stick" said he and down he went upon his knees, his white hair glistening in the moonlight and with hands clasped he exclaimed: "This is the proudest moment of my life! God I thank Thee that I am an Englishman." *Log of the "Great Eastern"* for 1860.

The actual distance from Milford Haven, the Company's starting point, to Port Philip, is some 12,000 miles, if no ports be touched at. A speed of 15 knots, (or 18 miles) an hour, would take the Great Eastern to the gold colony in about 32 days, and a ship of this capacity can carry 12,000 tons of coals, quite sufficient, it is stated, for her consumption on the outward and homeward voyages. In order to compensate for the loss of weight caused by enormous consumption of fuel, and to maintain an emersion of the paddles the coal will to a certain extent be replaced by water pumped into the water-tight compartments forming the skin of the ship.

At New York.

The number of persons who visited the ship on her first voyage to New York was 164,754, realizing about $83,296, or nearly £17,000. The greatest number in one day was 16,817, and the least 1,627 persons.

The *New York Herald* says:—The Great Eastern has had a favorable time in this country. She has cleared thousands of dollars since her arrival, and if she should remain here for a few months, she will clear many thousands more. This is the great theory of the "big ship."

The Great Eastern in the Mersey.

The following note of the voyage of the Great Ship appeared in the *Daily Post* of 5th June, 1861. It is from the pen of Mr. George Vandenhoff, Junr., son of the distinguished tragedian, and himself a cultivated disciple of Thespis.

The writer has for many years given up the stage and practised the law in the United States. It may be added that this is a return to his " old love," as he was, when quite a young man, Solicitor to the Mersey Dock Board :

The Great Eastern.

A NOTE OF THE VOYAGE. FROM GEO. VANDENHOFF, ESQ.

You tell me a few notes jotted down about our passage might interest your readers. I give you what I dotted down at the time.

Sat., 1st June. Lat. 49.30, Long. 21.11 W.—Here we are, seven days out from New York, 450 miles from Cape Clear, going along at the rate of fourteen knots an hour, as smoothly and steadily, and with as little sensation of movement as if we were seated in the easiest-going carriage, patent springs and axles, in the world, on the best and levellest of Macadamized roads. And the fact is, that the Great Eastern *has* macadamised the sea—taken all its ruts and rolling ground out of it—made it as even as a carpet, and entirely done away with all the " ups and downs " of the Atlantic Ocean travel. Sea sickness is no more ; squeamishness, and before breakfast qualms are unknown ; no man, " nor woman either," is in *Trinculo's* case any more, for *every one's* stomach is constant ; and the only danger is, that the whole of the company's profit on the passage may be devoured and swallowed up by the insatiable and never-by-any-chance-failing appetites of the " robustious " passengers. Sea air, you know, is a great tonic ; but, *en revanche*, there has always till now been sea-sickness to counterbalance the stomachic effect of the air, by the anti-stomachic " effect defective " of the jerkings and jumpings of

" The labouring bark,"

as she

" Climb'd hills of seas Olympus high,
And duck'd again as low as hell's from heaven ! "

But the Great Eastern has *changé tout cela*—she neither climbs nor ducks ; but goes on smoothly on her even way, really *ruling the waves*, and fulfilling the retching and wretched schoolmaster's aspiration—*ruling them straight*, too—while they play and ripple round her giant and impregnable sides with no more effect on her motion than the water of a pond has upon the plumage of a duck. She is as dry as a drawing room : there is no time at which her long and magnificent deck is at all wet—she does not ship a spoonful of sea ; consequently eating and drinking seem the great purpose of life, on board : there are no defaulters—there has not been one, I believe, from the beginning of the passage, at dinner, breakfast, or supper table. The only chance the company have of making up their deficit on the eatables, is by the proportionate consumption of drinkables ; and the perpetual popping of champagne corks gives some promise that so the balance may be restored.

In sober serious...ess, this is my twentieth passage across the Atlantic. I have done it by sail and by steam, and I never dreamed that it was possible to be really comfortable at sea; but the Great Eastern has proved that a passage across the Atlantic may be made a mere pleasure trip of nine or ten days. Fog was in our way for the first three days, and, of course, caution was advisable; less for our own sakes than for the sake of any vessels, large or small, that might be in our course; for even a light bump from our monster ship would knock the brains out of any ordinary craft; so, of course, we could not give her head at first. But, for the last three days we have had fine clear weather, and we make about 340 miles in every twenty-four hours, and "no one hurt!" "Think of that Master Brooke!" Nearly 15 miles an hour, as dry as a biscuit, and as easy as a carriage—and easier! But she has a *roll*, they say, True; she does roll a little, with the wind and sea a beam; otherwise she is perfectly steady But the roll, when it takes place, is a long roll (as long as a *French roll*), with no jerk in it; there is none of that kicking, diaphragmatic action that sends your heart and sometimes your dinner into your mouth. In fact it is a long, pleisurely, stately kind of a roll, that, as a fellow passenger says, acts on him as a kind of lullaby and calms him to sleep. Now this roll, which is only felt at all with wind and sea a beam—not at all with a head wind—is her only fault; and I learn that the managers of the vessel have by the last two trips gained such a perfect experience that they now feel quite confident by an improved system of stowage of her cargo, to obviate the difficulty entirely, so that there will not be a single *roll* on a passage, except the excellent ones that comes at breakfast every morning from the steward's pantry; and thus you may cross the Atlantic with no more danger of *mal de mer*, or of any other *mal*, than in crossing the ferry to Birkenhead.

Besides, we have got up a theatre—the Atlantic Theatre—on board; and last night the following entertainment—under the immediate direction and superintendence of your humble servant (to use the language of the play bills)— was given, to the great satisfaction and high delight of a suffocatingly-crowded audience, as witnessed by their enthusiastic applause. I send you a copy of the bill for the guidance and encouragement of future Ocean Thespians.

ATLANTIC THEATRE—GREAT EASTERN.
By permission and under the patronage of Neptune and the Sea Deities, Mermaids, &c.

THIS EVENING (FRIDAY), 31ST MAY, 1861.

The following Entertainment will be given, for the Benefit of the Widow of James Pollard, sailor.

Ouverture—Medley of American airs .... By the Orchestra.
Aria—"The heart bowed down" .... H. Lawrence, Esq.

Medley Song —" Alonzo the brave "..................W. Jones, Esq.
A Dance...........................By Monsieur Jack Tarre.
Hamlet's Solliloquy....................Richard W. Curtis, Esq.
Concertina Solo......................Walter Jones, Esq.
Comic Recitation..............Lieut. J. J. Cousins, 7th Y. V.
Irish Song.........................J. Harrison, Esq.
Recitative ed Aria —" Death of Nellson ".........W. Jones, Esq.
Treble Hornpipe......................By the Corps de Ballet.
Ethiopian Quintette ....Great Eastern Ministrels.
Finale—Medley of British airs..............By the Orchestra.

Tickets, 50c. or 2s. each. To be had at the Bar only.

Doors open at Eight o'clock. Performance to commence at Half past eight.

Well, everything went off admirably—not a mistake, not a kitche of any kind! Everybody was applauded, everybody was called, everybody was encored, everybody was pleased; and the proceeds, for the widow of a deserving fellow who lost his life on the last passage, exceeded $60, in addition to about $200 collected at the time of his death, and $100 promised by the proprietors.

We shall probably see Cape Clear to-morrow afternoon, about five o'clock, and hope to be in Liverpool on Monday. If everything holds out as it has done so far, it will have been the easiest and the pleasantest passage I shall have ever made.

The great fact to be noted is *the total absence of that terrible plague, sea-sicknsss, on Board the Great Eastern.* If she remain in the line between New York and Liverpool, that alone must make her the " pet of the petticoats;" and she is *par excellence* a *family vessel*, from the great space and comfortable arrangements of her state rooms, in which a family, with children and servants, can be accommodated *ensuite*. I must add that she is the sweetest and best ventilated vessel I ever sailed or steamed in.

Sunday I had the honour of reading the service on board, in consequence of the illness (land illness, not sea sickness) of the clergyman on board, and the whole of that day and night we had a pretty smart gale ahead, with rather a fierce sea running. But the good ship behaved splendidly; very little motion was felt (barring the " lullaby roll " aforesaid), and we made the Light shortly after nine o'clock, only about 24 hours after the Africa, that left New York three days before us.

It was really splendid to see how old Liverpool had turned out by water and land; how piers, and walls, and tugs, and ferry boats were crowded and decorated to welcome the arrival in our port of the great nautical wonder of her day: it was like the triumphant entry of a conquering hero.

Your's truly,
GEO. VANDENHOFF.

From the moment when the Great Eastern anchored in the Mersey, says the *Liverpool Journal,* she has been an object of the liveliest interest to our townspeople and to thousands who have been attracted from other localities. It has long been looked upon as a foregone conclusion that the greatest ship in the world must come to the greatest port; and now that their wishes are gratified by her presence, the people of the good old town have given no half-hearted welcome to the object of their admiration. Every day the river steamers which pass her moorings have been crowded, and the number of persons who have availed themselves of the opportunity to board and inspect the ship has been so far very large. To attempt any description of the Great Eastern would be superfluous after the countless histories and descriptions of the ship which have been published since she was launched at Blackwall. Besides, we doubt very much if any written description could convey to an intending visitor an adequate idea of the appearance and dimensions of the most stupendous vessel ever built. All previously acquired information is forgotten in the sensations of wonder and astonishment which the first sight of the Great Eastern will most certainly arouse; and even practical men, who have spent half a lifetime at sea—men who command our noble American and Australian liners—find themselves completely at a loss when they attempt to compare this magnificent vessel with any others previously existing. As the ship steamed up the river she passed the City of Baltimore, a very large and noble screw steamer, but which, on this occasion, was completely eclipsed by the dimensions and towering altitude of her neighbour. The Cunard steamer was dwarfed by the contrast to the dimensions of a mere tender; and it seemed as if the Woodside Ferry boats, which audaciously made the "passage round" the Great Eastern, could have been stowed away in her maintops.

The visitor to the ship who may have the good fortune to be carried to the Sloyne by the smart tender, the Rover will feel, on approaching her colossal sides, an uncomfortable impression that he is shortly to be called upon to do something of a startlingly acrobatic character. Access by the ordinary ladder cannot for a moment be dreamt of, and it will be with a feeling of great relief that the town-bred visitor will find himself comfortably passing in through a port-hole which is conveniently opened on a level with the bridge of the tender. Once fairly on board the visitor must be left to his own impressions. One caution, however, is necessary, he must avoid getting lost. The facilities for losing one self are on the largest scale. The immense expanse of the flush deck, the number and depth of the hatchways, the vast intricacies of the saloons and berths, and the wonderful engineering departments, demand from those who attempt to explore them exertions in the accurate calculation of latitude and longitude to which the most difficult "observations" at sea are as nought.

To the ladies, who form a large proportion of the visitors, the splendid saloons and berths will, no doubt, offer the greatest attractions. Whilst, in the design and construction of the frame of the ship, the most splendid triumph of the art of the engineer has been achieved, the interior fittings, and notably the saloons, present an equally remarkable example of perfection in the decorative art. Richly gilded cornices, marble columns and mantelpieces, wainscotting, on which the skill of the painter and the carver has been lavished; mirrors which reflect on every side a thousand beautiful objects; pianos, luxurious couches, and carpets of the richest texture and design—all these present an *ensemble* which would embellish a palace, and which has certainly hitherto been unknown as accompanying marine architecture. Into these luxurious retreats surely the malific influence of *mal de mer* can never enter.

Those of the "other sex" who have a penchant for engineering, will find ample occupation in inspecting the engines, which are worthy of the magnificent frame in which they are placed. Statistics as to the dimensions of pistons, pumps and cylinders, would only serve to embarrass the reader; the curious in such matters will find all the information ready to hand in guide books innumerable. Viewing these enormous machines as they are at present, in glittering inactivity, will give the beholder a sufficiently forcible idea of the wonderful power which is latent in them; and he will no doubt come to the conclusion that when they are at work impelling the noble ship through the waves, the noiseless movements of their vast and symmetrical proportions must be indeed the true poetry of motion. One of the most admirable features in connection with these ponderous machines is the facility with which they are made to respond to the orders of the captain or the officer in charge of the deck. A telegraphic apparatus is connected from the bridge with all the stations of the engineers, and the most urgent orders can thus be instantly obeyed. This improvement is also carried out in connection with the steering of the ship. The great resistance to be overcome necessitates the employment of four steering wheels upon the same axis, and the orders to the eight men at the helm are conveyed by an admirable system of dial signals. The compasses, the production of our townsman, Mr. John Gray, are splendid instruments, and have proved invaluable.

The population of the Great Eastern, supposing her to carry no passengers, is something considerable, amounting as it does to above 400 individuals. The ship is, however, able to accommodate 800 first class, 2,000 second class, and 1,200 third class passengers; besides having ample space for the stowage of coals (of which, when she is at sea, she consumes 300 tons a day), and an enormous cargo. A visit to this splendid ship cannot fail to impress every one with profound admiration of the genius that designed, and the skill and perseverance which completed such a structure. The Great Eastern, however unsuccessful hitherto in a pecuniary sense, is a ship which will be regarded with unabated interest and pride long after the fleet of which she is the pioneer have carried our flag in every sea.

On Saturday about 1,300 persons visited the ship, and on Monday as a consequence of the reduced charge for admission, the number increased, to 3,500. On Tuesday there were 1,680 visitors, and this number would doubtless have been largely increased but for the extremely unfavourable weather. On Thursday there were about 7,000 visitors to the vessel. Special trips have been organised in Manchester and the large towns in the county, and several thousand persons have been conveyed to Liverpool by these trips in order to avail themselves of the favourable opportunity to visit the great ship.

The largest number of visitors in one day was 17,000.

The Great Eastern chartered by Government.

The stay of the ship at this port will not be so long as was at first anticipated, for we learn that Government on Monday chartered the Great Eastern to convey two regiments of the line, comprising about 2,000 men, besides horses, to Quebec. Major Penn's No. 4 Battery, 4th Brigade Royal Artillery, now at Aldershott, was ordered to hold itself in readiness for immediate departure by this vessel. It is thought that the Great Eastern will sail from Liverpool in about a fortnight.

The "big ship" will be closed to the public after to day, when Messrs. John Laird, Sons, and Co., of the Birkenhead ironworks, will proceed to fit her up for the voyage. The Great Eastern will take out 2,144 officers and men, 473 women and children, and 122 horses, which will consist of the fourth field battery of Royal Artillery, consisting of 7 officers, 220 men, 20 women, 25 children, and 110 horses; the 30th Regiment; the 4th Battalion of the 60th Rifles; and 4 officers, 102 men, 9 women, and 19 children belonging to various detachments of the Royal Artillery, 16th Regiment, 17th Regiment, 100th Regiment, and Canadian Rifles. The 30th Regiment, and the 4th Battalion of the 60th Rifles, each comprise 39 officers, 868 men, 80 women, 120 children, and 6 horses. The screw-steamer Golden Fleece sailed from Liverpool on Thursday to embark at Dublin the 47th Foot, which is under orders for Canada. The fourth battery of the 4th Brigade of Artillery is commanded by Major

Penn. The following officers are attached to the battery, viz, second captain, J. J. Smith; lieutenants, R. J. Walker, T. M. Hitchins, and R. K. Young. The artillery force at present stationed in British North America consists of four batteries of the 7th Brigade, two of which are at Quebec and two at Halifax.

She Sails for Canada.—Her Captain.

The Great Eastern, under the able command of Capt. Kennedy, sailed from Liverpool on the 27th June, laden with troops for Canada. The ovation on her departure far exceeded that of her arrival. There were tens of thousands lining the quays and docks, who, as the Great Eastern glided majestically passed, with her decks covered with troops—the military bands playing fore and aft—thundered forth their good wishes to the Monarch of the Deep, which were returned with renewed vigor from her thousands of passengers and booming guns, presenting such a spectacle altogether unparallelled in the annals of maritime triumph.

Capt. Jas. Kennedy is quite a young man, apparently not more than 30 years of age. This is not only his first trip in command of the magnificent vessel, but his first trip to the St. Lawrence. On taking command of his vessel, Capt. Kennedy resolved to handle her in just the same way as an ordinary vessel, and brought her across without the slightest difficulty, until the pilots took her in charge and skilfully took her into port. We may here observe that she swings freely with the tide; and this was a point upon which some persons entertained doubts until they saw it effected. There is ample room, in her present berth, for three vessels of her size to swing with ease and safety—thus affording another proof of the superiority of the harbour of Quebec over any other into which the great ship has hitherto called.

Abstract of the Log.

June 27th, 1 p. m., left Liverpool, 28th, distance run up to noon, 300 miles; 29th, do. 302 do.; 30th, do. 318 do.; July 1st, do. 321; 2nd, do. 340 do.: at 4 a. m. passed R. M. S. "Arabia," bound east, lat. 50 N. long. 41 W., calm and dense fog throughout the day; passed several icebergs; 3rd, distance run, 320 miles; passed several icebergs; dense fog all day. 4th, 8 p. m., sighted Cape Pine Light; 9 p. m., dense fog; standing by the engines, owing to so many vessels being in our track; passed the American ship "Lizzy Southard," bound in; also the ship "Almeira," (2nd distinguishing pendant 4507.) 5th, distance run, 320 miles; 8 p, m., St. Paul's Island abeam; passed several vessels; 2,30 p. m., passed S. S. "John Bell." 6th, arrived off Quebec at 7 p. m.

Throughout the voyage moderate weather and smooth water, but dense fog from 29th June up to 5th July.

The Great Eastern was exactly eight days from the pilot was discharged at Liverpool till the pilots were taken on board at Point des Monts, and during all this time there were but 20 hours of clear weather. Cape Race was made in six days from Liverpool, but it was too thick to communicate with the shore.

Printed in Poland
by Amazon Fulfillment
Poland Sp. z o.o., Wrocław